Letter

-in, -ig, -it

 Harcourt
SCHOOL PUBLISHERS

ISBN-13: 978-0-15-358372-8
ISBN-10: 0-15-358372-X

Ordering Options
ISBN 10: 0-15-358355-X (Grade K Below-Level Collection)
ISBN 13: 978-0-15-358355-1 (Grade K Below-Level Collection)
ISBN 10: 0-15-360625-8 (package of 5)
ISBN 13: 978-0-15-360625-0 (package of 5)

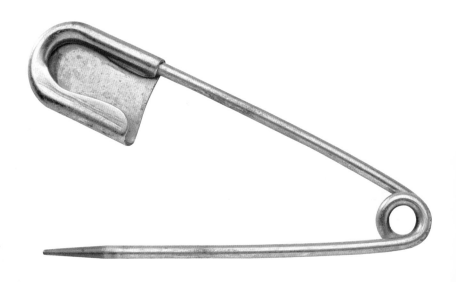

pin

pig

pit

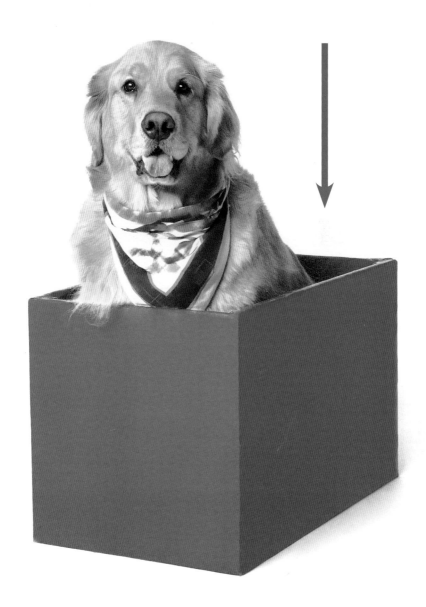

in

dig

fin

sit